This book may be kept

Arab Public Library

20025433

D1708903

J746.14 20025433
RUB   Rubenstone, Jessie.
         Weaving for beginners   .00

WEAVING FOR BEGINNERS

ARAB PUBLIC LIBRARY

J
746.14
Rub

WEAVING FOR BEGINNERS

by Jessie Rubenstone

Photographs by Charles Forbes Ward, Jr.

J. B. Lippincott Company / Philadelphia and New York

Mumford 1/79   3.48

For Nancy — a model girl

The author wishes to thank Robert F. Stafford, Professor Emeritus of Textile Design, Philadelphia College of Textiles and Science, for his valuable assistance as a consultant.

Thanks to members of the Philadelphia Guild of Handweavers, Rilla "Sam" Banbury, and Eva Van de Pol for their interest and cooperation. Thanks also to Mrs. Harry M. Keating of Lee, Massachusetts, member of the Weavers' Guild of the Southern Berkshires, for the delightful visit I spent with her.

Thanks to Martha Fuhrman for typing the manuscript.

Thanks to Frances Finkelstein, a willing friend, who tested the instructions.

Copyright © 1975 by Jessie Rubenstone
All rights reserved
Printed in the United States of America
First Edition

U.S. Library of Congress Cataloging in Publication Data

Rubenstone, Jessie.
Weaving for beginners.

SUMMARY: An introduction to the equipment and techniques of weaving with instructions for making such items as a shag rug, shoulder bag, scarf, and a pillow.

1. Hand weaving—Juvenile literature. [1. Weaving. 2. Handicraft] I. Ward, Charles Forbes. II. Title
TT848.R8   746.1'4   75-16309
ISBN-0-397-31635-6   ISBN-0-397-31636-4 (pbk.)

Contents

So You Want to Weave

Weaving is how fabric (cloth) is made. Two sets of threads* are interlaced at right angles. What does this mean? Look at the material in something you are wearing. You will be able to see some threads that go from top to bottom and other threads that cross them. If the material is a knit, you will not see these two sets of threads because knitted material is made from one continuous thread.

Perhaps you have already done some weaving. You may have made something by putting one piece of paper or some other material over and under other pieces.

*In this book "thread" does not mean sewing thread. A thread is a piece of yarn, string, or any other material being used in weaving.

5

If you go over a thread on the first row, you will go under that thread on the next row. Suppose we had to use a needle to go under and over each thread in order to weave fabric. It would not be even or straight. It would take years to make a piece of material, and nobody could afford to buy it.

So how is it done? What is the secret of getting evenly woven material that we can buy at moderate prices?

The secret is a *loom*. A loom is a device that holds the threads tight and raises and lowers a whole set of these threads at one time. These are the threads that run the long way in the material (the *warp*). The loom makes it easy to put the crosswise thread (the *weft*) over and under the warp threads.

In this book you will learn to make a loom with very simple materials, and you will learn to weave. The principle of weaving is the same whether it is done on the simple loom you will use or on a big power loom in a weaving factory or mill.

One of the exciting things about weaving is the variety of materials that can be used. All kinds of string and yarn with their range of colors and textures will make many beautiful combinations. But other kinds of materials may be used as well. The articles in this book have been made from wool, cotton, rayon, etc., even from used plastic bags and an old pair of blue jeans. Weavers do not waste materials. You may have a piece of clothing that is out of style or worn out. If you cut the good parts of the garment into strips, you will be able to weave it into something you will continue to enjoy. You will also be able to use the threads that are left on the loom after the fabric is cut off. These leftover threads are called *thrums.* The shag rug on p. 53 was made with thrums.

Do not expect your weaving to look perfect. Only weaving that is done on a machine will look perfect. Part of the beauty and interest of handweaving is that it does not look perfect. As you practice, your weaving will become more even.

What You Will Need

WEAVING MATERIALS

In weaving you will use both string and yarn. String and yarn are made by a process called *spinning* in which tiny threads called *fibers* are twisted together. If you untwist an end of string or yarn, you will see two, three, or four separate threads. These are called *ply*. Untwist one of these thin threads. You will see the fine fibers that were twisted (spun) together to make the thread. Early settlers in this country did their spinning by hand, and people in many other countries still do handspinning, but nearly all of the string and yarn made today is spun on machines in factories.

There are many different kinds and weights (thicknesses) of string and yarn, depending on the type of fibers used and the number of ply. You can use almost any kind to learn to weave, but later when you begin a weaving project, be sure you select the right type of yarn for the article you are going to weave. Heavy string and rug yarn would be good for making a rug but not for making a scarf.

Before you buy string or yarn, it is important to read the label. It will give you some or all of the following information:

Fiber. This may be cotton, wool, silk, rayon, nylon, Acrilan, etc. Cotton, wool, and silk are *natural* fibers; they are found in nature. The others are made in factories and are called *synthetic* fibers. Many synthetic fibers look and feel like the natural fibers.

String is usually made from cotton. Some yarns are made from combinations of fibers. String and yarn made from any of these fibers or combinations of fibers are good to use for weaving. Remember that yarn that contains any wool must be washed in cold water.

Amount. Yarn labels usually give the weight in ounces. String labels give the length in feet or yards.

Ply. Yarn labels usually show the number of ply. Heavy yarn (three or more ply) is best to use in weaving, especially for beginners.

Dye lot. Skeins of yarn with the same dye lot number were all dyed at the same time. Even if two skeins of yarn are the same color, they will be a little different if they were not dyed in the same dye lot. Buy all the yarn for a project at the same time to make sure it will all be the same color. If you want to use stripes or a mixture of colors, you can sometimes get bargains on odds and ends of yarn.

String is the material most often used for the warp (the lengthwise threads that are put into the loom first) because it is usually stronger than yarn, and these threads must be strong. String is sold in balls. A good kind of string to start with is the ordinary white household string used to tie packages.

Yarn is most often used for the weft (the crosswise threads). Yarn that is spun for weaving is firmer than knitting yarn. Knitting yarn is spun more loosely and is soft and fluffy. Both kinds can be used for weaving. If you want to use yarn for the warp, check to see that it does not break easily when you pull it between your hands.

Yarn is usually sold in *skeins*. Yarn in a "pull skein" will come out easily. Yarn in a regular skein or *hank* (a loose coil of yarn) must be rolled into balls before using or it will become tangled. Open the hank. Place it over the back of a chair or over a friend's two hands. Wind the yarn *loosely* into balls.

Because the weft does not need to be as strong as the warp, almost any kind of material can be used. Instead of using a single thread, try using several, either the same or a mixture of colors and textures. You can also work with strips of cloth or strips cut from plastic bags.

THE LOOM

A loom is a device that holds the warp threads tight and raises and lowers them. The part that raises and lowers the warp threads is a frame called a *harness*. You will make a harness before you begin to weave.

To hold the warp threads tight, you can tie the back end of the warp to anything that is sturdy and will not move, like a doorknob or a bedpost. You will need another firm place to fasten the front end of the warp. Try tying the front end to the side of a chair and sit on the chair to weave. Your weight will keep the chair from moving.

The photographs in this book show the weaving attached between two posts. These posts are part of the *beginner loom* made from the diagram on p. 76. It works well for small articles and lets you do your weaving wherever you wish. Later you may want to make this or something like it.

OTHER SUPPLIES

Sticks. You will need sticks to make the harness and to use as warp sticks. The sticks to use are flat wooden sticks. They are called Popsicle sticks, ice-cream sticks, craft sticks, slapsticks, coffee stirrers, and probably other names. They measure $4\frac{1}{2}$ inches long and $\frac{3}{8}$ inch wide. You can buy them, or you may save the sticks from ice-cream bars. If you buy the sticks, you will get a few for a penny, but they are usually sold only in large quantities. They are sold in hobby shops and in some five-and-ten-cent stores. To use sticks from ice-cream bars, wash them in cold water and dry them. It is a good idea to weight them down with a heavy book to keep them flat as they dry.

Tape measure or *yardstick* for measuring warp.

Comb for beating. Choose a comb with teeth that are spaced far apart. If the teeth are close together, they may fray the yarn.

Tapestry needle. This is a heavy sewing needle with a large eye and a blunt point.

Ruler, scissors, string, masking tape, crochet hook, knitting needle or *pointed dowel, straight pins* and *safety pins.*

For making the harness you will also need a drill or some string, plus glue, a pencil, and sandpaper.

First Steps

KNOTS

Learning to tie knots is an important part of learning to weave. The following knots will be used in warping the loom, in preparing the weft, and in finishing off the warp ends after the weaving is completed. If you make a harness with string *heddles* (vertical sticks or strings used to raise and lower warp threads), you will use some of these knots. Practice making the knots until you can do them easily. You will find other uses for them outside of weaving.

Overhand knot. This "single knot" is the first step in making other knots. It is also used alone.

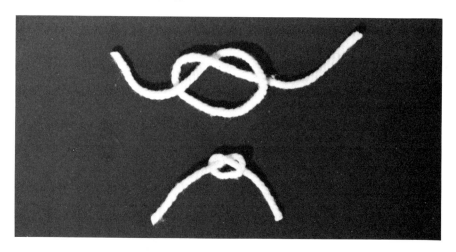

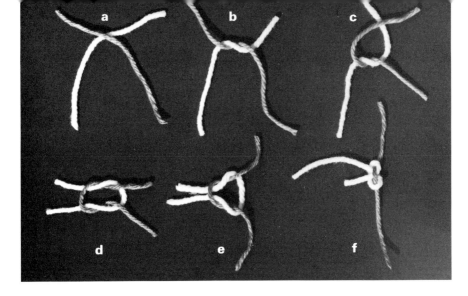

Square knot. Use two colors of yarn for practice.

(*a*) Place dark color yarn on top of light color.

(*b*) Tie an overhand knot.

(*c*) Put dark color on top again.

(*d*) Tie another overhand knot. The picture shows the square knot before it is tightened. Pull it tight. It will lie flat.

(*e*) Even though it is a strong knot, the square knot can be pulled apart easily. Take the two ends of the dark yarn and pull them out straight. (It works the same with the light yarn.)

(*f*) Pull the knot along the dark yarn and it will slide off.

Half bowknot. This knot is easy to pull apart and tie again. You may also use a bowknot, pulling through two folds as you do in tying your shoelace.

(*a*) Tie an overhand knot (arrow). Tie another overhand knot, but this time fold one end and pull it through.

(*b, c*) Pull it tight.

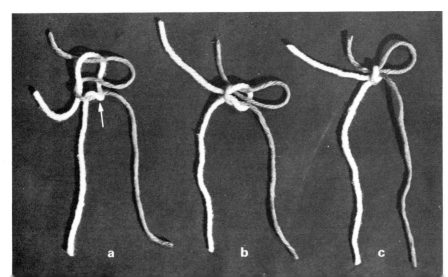

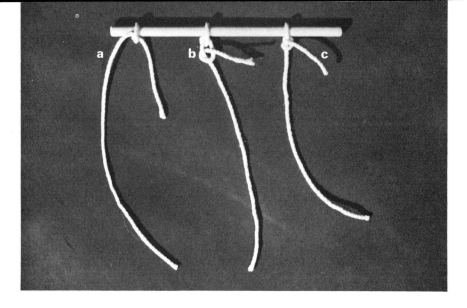

Two half hitches. When an overhand knot is tied to a stick, it is called a half hitch.

(*a*) Tie an overhand knot on a stick.

(*b*) Take the short end and tie another overhand knot, making sure the end comes out between the two knots.

(*c*) Pull tight.

Snitch knot. This is also called "lark's head."

(*a*) Fold string in half and lay a stick across it.

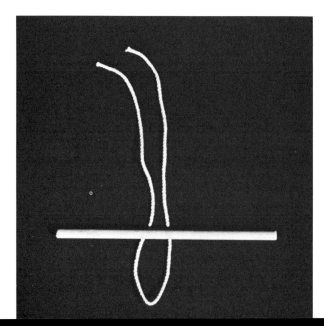

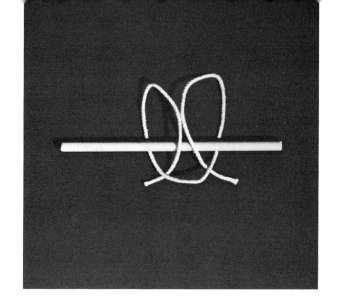

(b) Pull cut ends through the loop formed by the fold.

(c) Pull cut ends to tighten.

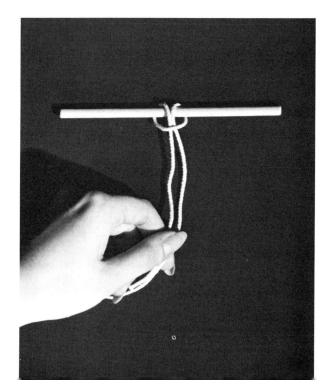

MAKING A HARNESS

To make a harness, you will need the equipment shown in the picture. A harness can have stick heddles or string heddles. Both kinds work well.

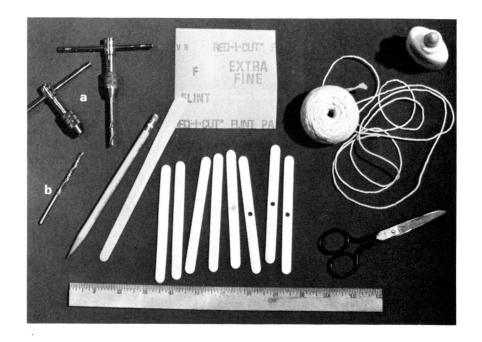

Drill. For stick heddles, you will need a drill to make holes in the sticks. Perhaps you have or can borrow a drill of some kind. If not, you can buy a drill for about $1.50 at a hardware store. Buy a tap wrench (*a*), which will cost about $1.00, and a drill bit (*b*) size 11/64. Buy the tap wrench and the drill bit at the same time so you can be sure the bit will fit into the wrench. Tighten the tap wrench until it holds the drill bit firmly. You may need to use a pair of pliers for this. You will not need the drill if you make the string harness.

String. For making string heddles only.

Sticks. For a harness with stick heddles, you will need thirteen of the sticks described on p. 11. For the harness with string heddles, you will need six sticks.

Glue. White glue, such as Elmer's. It is strong and dries clear.

Pencil.

Sandpaper. One sheet, grade fine or extra fine. It will cost about ten cents. Only a small piece is needed. For easy use, tape a piece of sandpaper along a flat stick. An emery board may be used instead.

HARNESS WITH STICK HEDDLES

1. Find the center points of 9 sticks by measuring each with a ruler. Mark centers with a pencil. Drill a hole in the center of each stick. Use sandpaper to get the sticks smooth.
2. Using a sheet of paper as a guide to keep the sticks straight, put one stick without a hole along the edge of the paper (*a*) and another stick (*b*) parallel to it 4½ inches away.

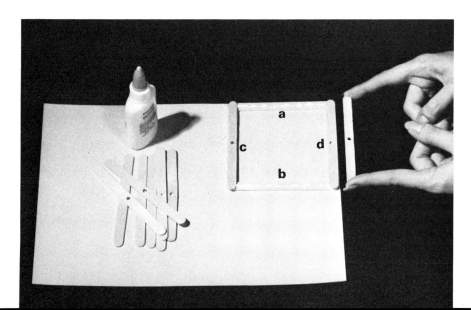

3. Squeeze a thin line of glue down the center of each of these sticks.

4. Form a square by placing 2 sticks with holes (*c, d*) across the ends of the first sticks. When placing the sticks you will have good control if you hold them, as shown in the picture, with your two forefingers. If the corner matches the corner of the paper, it will be square.

5. Place the other 7 sticks with holes evenly along the first sticks. Try to keep them the same distance apart.

6. Put a drop of glue at both ends of each stick.

7. Place a stick across the glue dots at the top (*e*) and another at the bottom (*f*). Allow glue to set for about ten minutes.

8. Put a piece of paper on top of the harness. Place a heavy book on top and leave it till the glue dries (about two hours). Be careful not to move the sticks.

9. With a pencil, make a small arrow at each end of the center stick. These marks will show the center of the harness. Mark center arrows on both front and back of harness.

Even if you have been careful, you may find that all the eyes (holes) in your harness are not exactly in the center. This is all right. Your weaving will be just as good even if they are not perfectly centered.

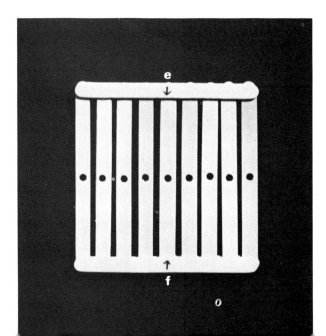

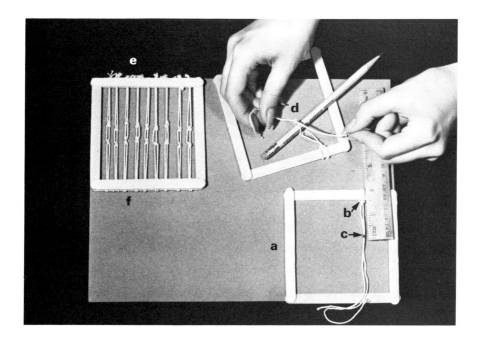

1. Using a sheet of paper as a guide to keep the sticks straight, place one stick along the edge and another stick parallel to it, 4½ inches away.

2. Put a drop of glue at both ends of both sticks and put two more sticks on top to form a square (a). If the corner matches the corner of the paper, it will be square. Let the glue set for about ten minutes. Place a piece of paper and then a book on top of the sticks. Let dry for two hours.

3. Cut nine pieces of string 16 inches long.

4. Fold one piece of string in half and fasten it to one of the sticks with a snitch knot (b).

5. Measure down 1½ inches on the string. Mark this spot and tie a square knot (c).

6. Place a pencil on the square knot between the ends of string and tie another square knot over it (d). This forms the eye of the heddle.

7. Tie the heddle to the stick at the other side of the harness with a square knot.

8. Tie the other eight heddles the same way. Try to get the eye in the middle of each heddle.

9. Put a line of glue along each of the sticks holding the strings. Put another stick on top of the glue (e, f). Allow glue to set for about ten minutes.

10. Put a piece of paper on top of the harness. Place a heavy book on top and leave it till the glue dries (about two hours).

Practice Piece

WARPING THE LOOM

1. Measure the warp (also called "warp threads" and "warp ends"). For the practice piece, cut 17 pieces of string or yarn 36 inches (1 yard) long. Learning this step will be easier if you use two different colors. Cut 9 pieces of a dark color and 8 pieces of a light color.

2. Tie ends of warp together with an overhand knot.

3. Tie this knot to something firm so that you can pull on it. A doorknob, a bedpost, or a heavy chair would be good, or there may be a strong hook in a wall that you can tie it to. If you can work outside, use a small tree trunk. The beginner loom (p. 76) may also be used. You can make the warp more secure by using masking tape (*a*) to hold the warp threads together.

    This end is called the back of the warp.

4. Comb through the warp threads to straighten them.

ARAB PUBLIC LIBRARY

14794

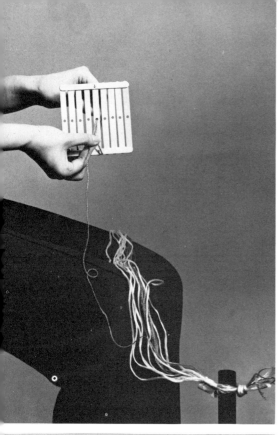

5. Put a chair near where you have tied the warp threads. Sit down and hold the harness in one hand.

To put the warp through the harness, start with one of the 9 dark threads. Fold back about 2 inches of the thread and push the folded end through the middle eye (hole).

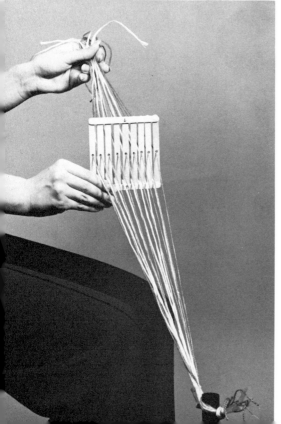

6. Next, put a light thread through a slit (space between the sticks). Continue to put a dark thread in each eye and a light one in each slit until all the threads are used.

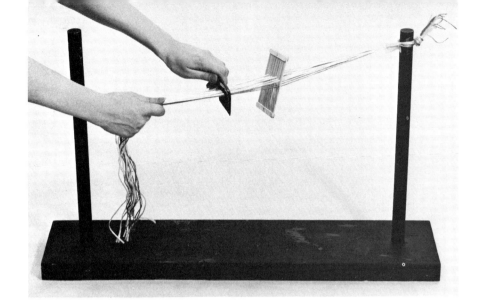

7. Holding all the ends in your hand, comb the warp again to make sure it is straight.

8. Fasten this front end of the warp together with an overhand knot or a piece of masking tape about one foot from the end of the threads. Divide these end threads into two bunches and tie them around another firm place with a half bowknot. It is important to keep the threads tightly stretched. If they get loose as you weave, untie the knot and tie it again tightly. Put your hand on top of the warp and press the threads lightly. They should all feel about the same tension (tightness).

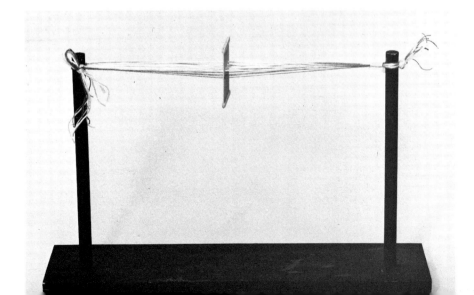

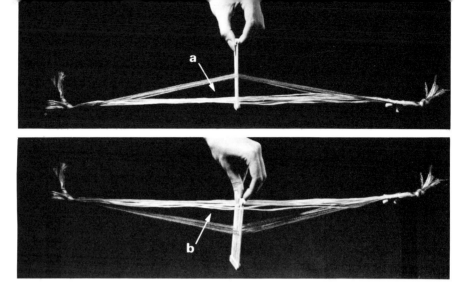

9. Raise the harness. The opening that is formed (*a*) is called a *shed*. Push the harness down. This forms the other shed (*b*). If you have used two colors of warp threads, all the same color will be on top when you raise the harness. When you push the harness down, the other color will be on top. Raising and lowering the harness is called *changing the shed*.

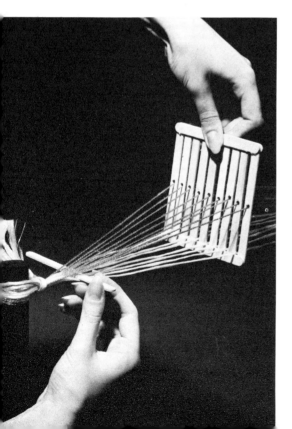

10. Raise the harness. Put a stick in this shed at the end of the warp nearest you (the front end). A stick used this way is called a *warp stick*. Warp sticks hold the warp threads in place and allow you to space the threads evenly.

11. Change the shed (lower the harness). Put a second warp stick in this shed.

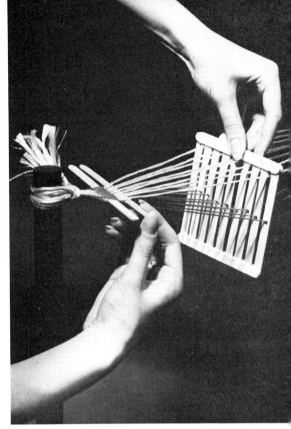

12. Change the shed. Put in a third warp stick.

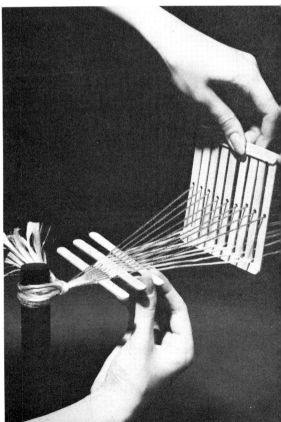

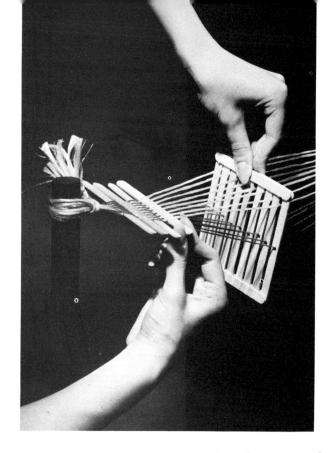

13. Change the shed. Put in a fourth warp stick.

Use a ruler to measure the width of the warp threads on the fourth stick. The warp will probably be 1 inch to 2 inches wide, depending on the kind of warp thread used. Whatever the measurement is, you should try to keep the width the same all the way along the weaving.

BUTTERFLY

The thread that goes across the warp is called the weft. Putting the weft through the shed is called *passing the weft*. You will be able to pass the weft easily if you wind it into a *butterfly*.

Instead of making a butterfly, you may wind the weft around a piece of cardboard to form a shuttle if you prefer. Wooden shuttles are also used in weaving. An antique wooden shuttle is shown in the picture on the title page of this book.

1. Cut a piece of yarn about 4 yards long. Put one end between your first and middle fingers, letting about 1 foot of yarn hang down the back of your hand.
2. Wind the other part of the yarn over your thumb and then over your little finger.

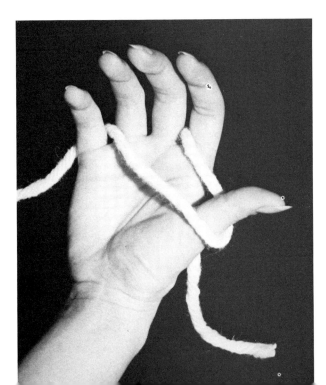

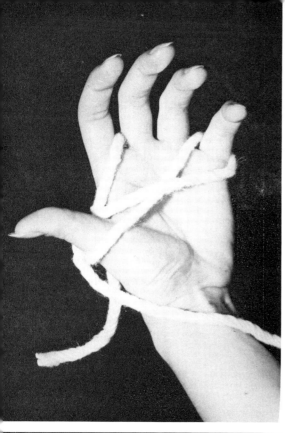

3. Bring it back up around your thumb to form a figure 8. Hold your hand open. Continue winding the yarn onto your hand in this figure-8 shape, leaving an end about 1 foot long.

4. Using this end, fasten the butterfly in the middle with two half hitches.

5. Remove it from your hand. The yarn will unwind easily if you pull the long piece that started at the back of your hand.

HOW TO WEAVE

Before you begin, be sure the warps are spread evenly on the fourth stick. Measure the width.

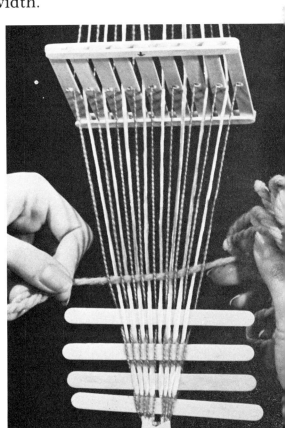

1. Raise the harness (open the shed), hold onto the butterfly, and put the end of the weft into this shed, leaving about 2 inches sticking out at the side.

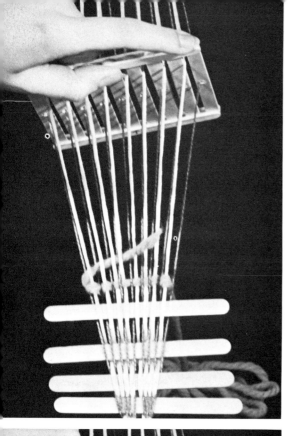

2. Change shed. Put the short end into this shed, bringing the end up between the warp threads about halfway across. This turns the end back into the weaving.

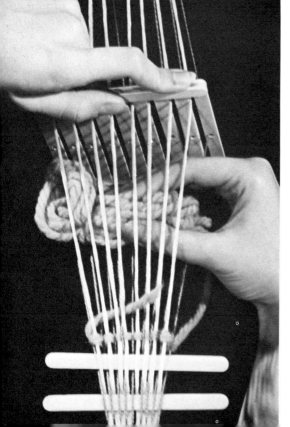

3. Pass the weft through the same shed. (The harness is still pushed down.) Use both hands to pass the weft, one to put it in at one side and one to pull it out through the other.

As you pull it through, slant the weft and hold onto both the weft and the end warp thread. This will prevent the edge of the fabric from pulling in.

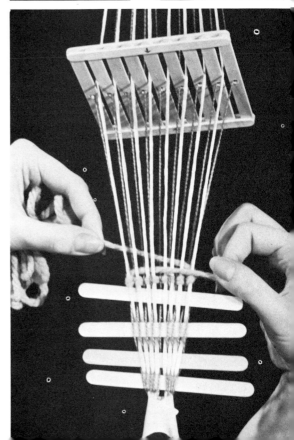

4. Hold onto the two ends and pull them until the warp is the same width that you measured on the fourth warp stick. Check with a ruler.

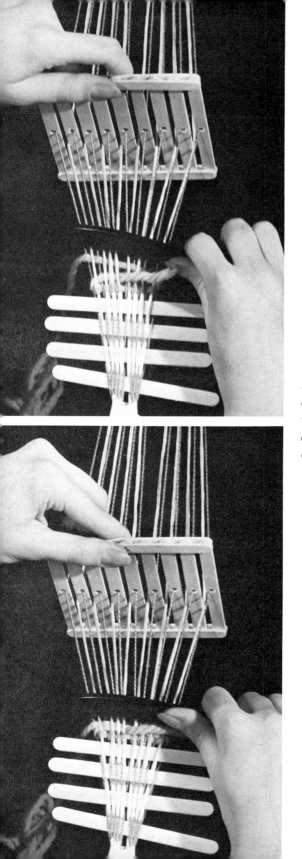

5. Change shed and *beat* by using a comb to press the weft down toward the warp sticks. Try to press the weft down evenly so that the fabric will be even.

6. Trim off the extra end of weft that was turned in.

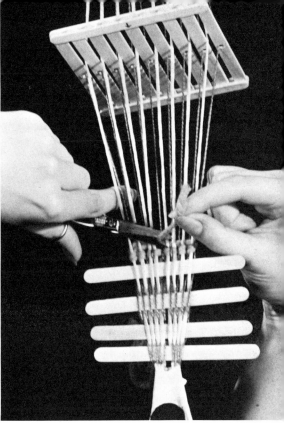

7. Pass the weft. Be sure to slant the weft and hold onto both the weft and the end warp.

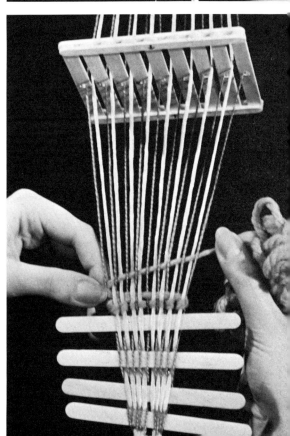

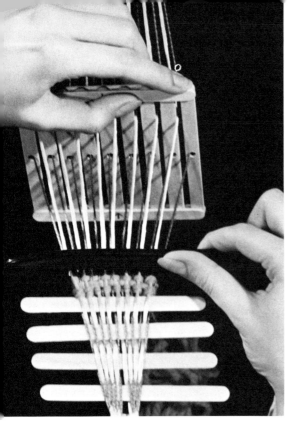

8. Change shed and beat.

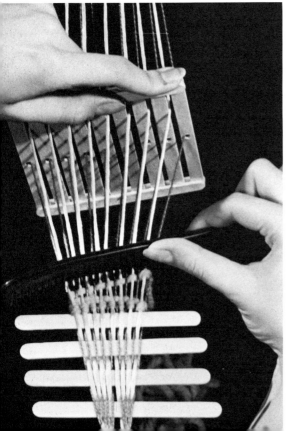

Continue to pass weft, change shed, and beat. You will soon see the fabric develop. Measure the fabric as you weave to make sure it is even. Measure the width, and measure the length along both sides. If one side is longer than the other, you are not beating evenly. To get a true measurement, push the harness away from the weaving.

Finish the weaving when you get near the end of the weft or when you get too close to the harness. You cannot work very close to the harness because the shed will not be high enough for the weft to pass.

9. To end the weaving, cut the weft, leaving an end about 2 inches long at the side. Turn this end back in by weaving it over and under at least three warp threads in the row *before* the last one, using your fingers or a crochet hook. Leave the end on top of the fabric.

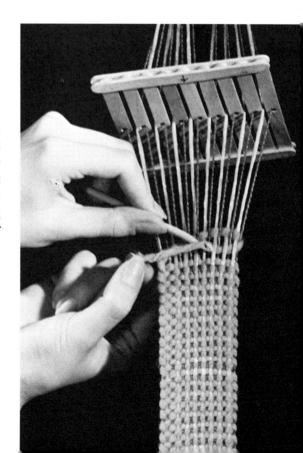

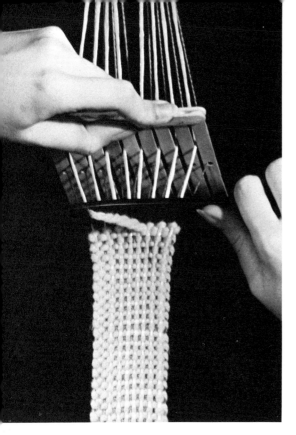

10. Change shed and beat. Trim off the end of the weft.

To remove the fabric from the loom, you will cut the warp threads. But before you cut the warp, look at your weaving. The end of your fabric probably looks better than the beginning. If you want to practice some more, you can use the same warp and weft. Open the shed and pull out the weft. Then change the shed and re-move the next row of weft. Continue to do this until it is all out and you are ready to start again. When you are satisfied with your weaving, go on to the next step.

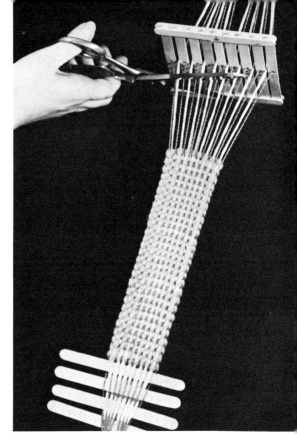

11. Cut the warp threads a few inches from each end of the weaving. Remove the warp sticks that were put in at the beginning. Tie the warp threads together to prevent the fabric from raveling and to form a fringe. Tie two threads together in a square knot, getting the knots as close to the fabric as possible. Trim the fringe evenly, measuring it with a ruler.

You do not need to do anything to the sides of the fabric to keep it from raveling. As the weft passes over the end warp it forms a "self edge" or *selvage* that finishes off the sides.

You now know how to weave. The kind of fabric that you have woven is called *plain weave* or *tabby.* It is the most common and the easiest to do. It will look different depending on how hard you beat the weft. If you press down hard, the weft will cover the warp. If you press lightly, the warp will show. Both ways are attractive.

Making the Sample

Now you are ready to make the sample. It includes plain weave, which you have already learned, and two other weaves, loop and knot. The sample may be used as a wall hanging. After you have made the sample, you will be able to make everything else in this book.

Prepare warp and butterfly the same as for the practice piece but measure 5 yards of yarn for the butterfly.

Work plain weave for 2 inches. End with weft at right.

LOOP

1. Pass the weft from right to left. Leave it loose; do not beat.

Use a knitting needle, a sharpened dowel, or a crochet hook to make the loops. Skip the first two warp threads on the right, put the point under the weft that lies on top of the third warp thread, and pull it up to form a loop on the needle.

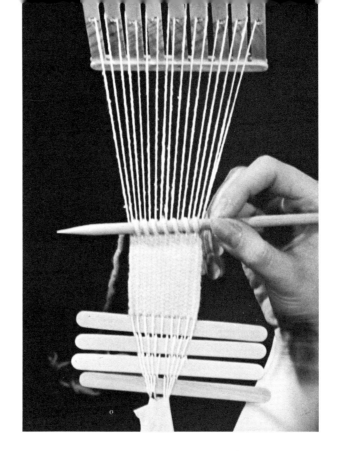

2. Skip the next warp thread and pick up another loop above the following warp thread. It will be easy to see where to pick up a loop, as the weft will be on top of the warp thread. Continue to pick up loops until you reach the end of the row. You will have seven loops on the needle.

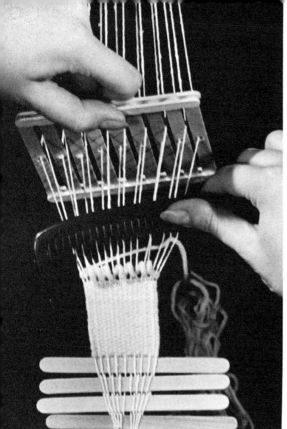 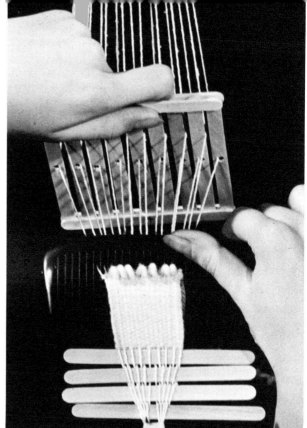

3. Change shed and pass the weft. Remember to slant the weft and to hold onto the weft and the end warp. Remove needle from loops. Change shed and beat.

Work two more rows of plain weave. The weft will be on the right, and you will be ready to repeat steps 1 through 3 for another row of loops. There should be three rows of plain weave between rows of loops. Continue until you have seven rows of loops.

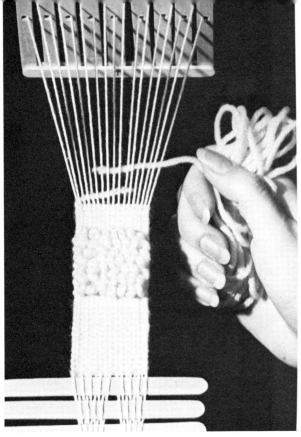
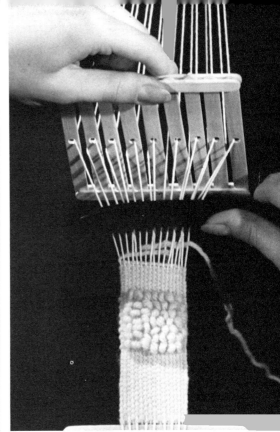

(a)   (b)

ADDING NEW WEFT: If you used 5 yards of yarn for your butterfly, you should have enough to finish the loops. But when you run out of weft, it is easy to add a new piece. Make another butterfly and put the end into the same shed, letting the new yarn run alongside the old yarn for about an inch (a). Change shed and beat (b).

KNOT

Work 1 inch of plain weave after the loops.

For the knots, cut 49 pieces of yarn about 3 inches long (red wool was used here) and 98 pieces of another color (green rayon was used here). The pieces may be measured with a ruler or by winding the yarn around a card 1½ inches wide and cutting along one side. Do not try to get them all exactly the same length because you want a shaggy effect.

The pieces of warp that are left on a loom when the fabric is cut away are called thrums. These also can be used for knots.

1. Skip the end warp thread. To make the first knot, put three pieces of yarn over the next two warp threads.

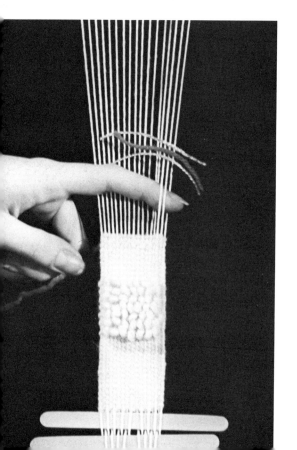

2. Pull the ends of these short pieces down and around these two warp threads, under, and then up between the two warp threads.

3. Slide the knot down to the fabric by pulling all the ends at one time.

Skip the next warp thread and repeat the knot in the following two warp threads. Continue to make knots until you reach the end of the row, skipping one warp thread before each knot. You will have five knots.

Change shed and plain weave for ½ inch, ending with warp at right.

Make a second row of knots. On the second row, skip the first two warp threads before making a knot. This will leave one warp thread at the end of the row instead of two, and the knots will look more even.

After the second row of knots, plain weave for ½ inch.

Change shed. Insert a stick. Change shed.

Plain weave for ½ inch (a new color was used here). As in the practice piece, begin and end the weft so that the ends are turned back into the fabric.

Cut the warp and remove the sample from the loom, leaving warp threads long enough to tie the fringe.

Tie square knots in the warp threads at the top and trim to about ½ inch.

Put the sample on a table with a book on top to hold it in place. Remove the warp sticks and tie the warp threads with overhand knots to form the bottom fringe, three threads at a time. Tighten each knot as you push it close to the fabric (a). Comb the fringe. Measuring with a ruler, trim it to 1½ inches.

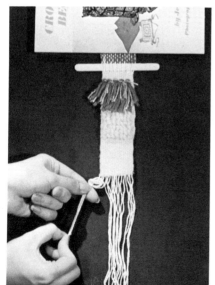

(a)

You have finished the sample. To use it as a wall hanging, tie a string to the ends of the stick.

You can now make all the articles in this book.

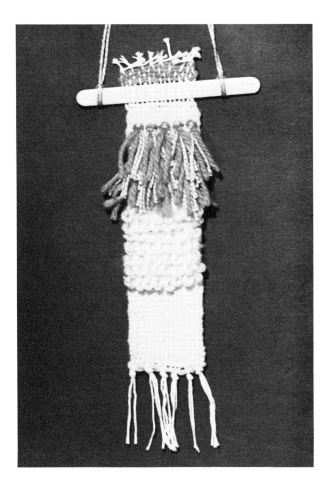

Articles to Weave

The instructions for making the articles pictured on the following pages will include the kind of yarn that was used, some idea of the amount of yarn needed, and the finished size.

It is not possible to be very accurate about amounts of weaving materials. Part of the warp is nearly always left on the loom, and you must allow for this loss when estimating the amount of yarn needed. Also, there is a large variety of weights and thicknesses of yarn. If your yarn is thinner than the yarn used to make the article in the picture, you will need more; if it is thicker or heavier, you will need less. It is not necessary to use the same yarn. Any kind of yarn or mixture of different kinds may be used. The "finished size" measurements will depend on the kind of yarn used.

Color suggestions are also included. If you use these colors, the finished articles will look like those in the pictures. But you may use any color or combination of colors that you like. Two or more colors woven together will produce a different effect than if only one color is used. If you use a red warp and a yellow weft, your weaving will look orange. Blue used with yellow will look green.

These sample projects are just a beginning. Once you have practiced your weaving by making them, you will be able to plan and design original weaving projects. There are many books on weaving, as well as articles in magazines and newspapers. You may also be able to get ideas from examples of handweaving at art exhibits, craft shows, and fairs.

BOOKMARK

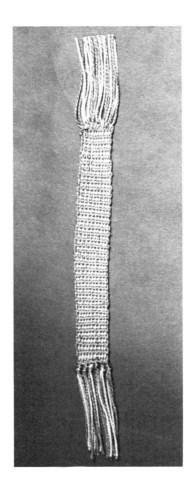

Warp: Rayon yarn (green and yellow)
        17 threads, 1 yard long
Weft: Rayon yarn (green)
Amount needed: Less than ½ ounce (total)
Finished size: 1¼ inches wide, 14 inches long (including fringe)

Warp the loom as you did for the practice piece, following directions on p. 21.

Plain weave for 8 inches.

Cut from loom, leaving about 5 inches of warp on each end for the fringe.

Tie the fringe with square or overhand knots and trim to 3 inches.

You can experiment with the bookmark. Make it narrower by using fewer warp threads. Make one or more rows of loops or knots at the top. Use warp threads of one color through the center and another color to form stripes at the sides. Braid the fringe, using three warp threads at a time, and finish with an overhand knot. Try using some of your own ideas.

HEADBAND

Warp: Rayon yarn (red and yellow)
      17 threads, 1 yard long
Weft: Rayon yarn (red)
Amounts needed: Less than ½ ounce red, less than ½ ounce yellow
Finished size: 1¼ inches wide, 36 inches long (including fringe)

Warp the loom, following directions on p. 21, but measure off about 10 inches of warp before putting in the warp sticks. This extra warp will be needed for the long fringe. Wind the extra warp around whatever the end of the warp is tied to.

Plain weave for 18 inches.

When removing the weaving from the loom, do not cut the warp. Just untie the knots at both ends and remove the harness.

Tie the fringe in square or overhand knots and trim it to about 10 inches.

To put on the headband, tie the fringe to make it the right size for your head.

BELT

Warp: Wool yarn (several colors were used)
      17 threads, 2 yards long
Weft: Wool yarn (white)
Amount needed: 1½ ounces for warp, ½ ounce white for weft
Finished size: 1½ inches wide, 2 yards long (including fringe)

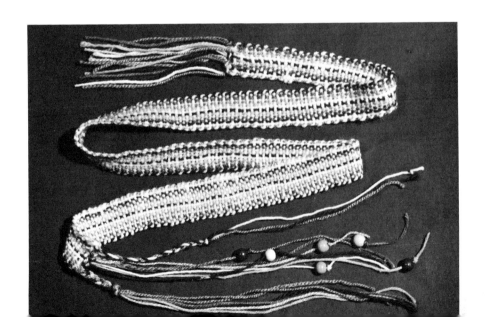

Warp the loom, following directions on p. 21.

Plain weave for 45 inches. As the belt gets longer, you may want to wind it around whatever the warp is attached to. Fasten it well with pins or with masking tape, so that the warp is stretched tightly. Or fold and pin it into place with safety pins (see p. 64). However, if you have a long space in which to stretch the warp, folding will not be necessary.

When removing the belt from the loom, do not cut the warp. Just untie the knots at both ends and remove the harness.

The belt can be finished in any of the styles shown in the picture.

For the short fringe shown at the top, tie overhand knots in the warp, three threads at a time.

For the thin braided fringe, braid three single warp threads together. Finish the braid with an overhand knot.

For fringe with beads, tie overhand knots, then add beads. To get the thread through the beads, put a small amount of glue along the end of the thread for about an inch and roll it tight between your fingers. When it hardens, you will have a "needle" to put through the beads.

For thick braided fringe (bottom), braid three double warp threads together, so that each braid contains six threads. End the braid with an overhand knot.

BELT WITH LONG FRINGE

Warp: Rayon yarn (red)
        17 threads, 2 yards long
Weft: Rayon yarn (red)
Amount needed: About 2 ounces
Finished size: 1¾ inches wide, 2 yards long (including fringe)

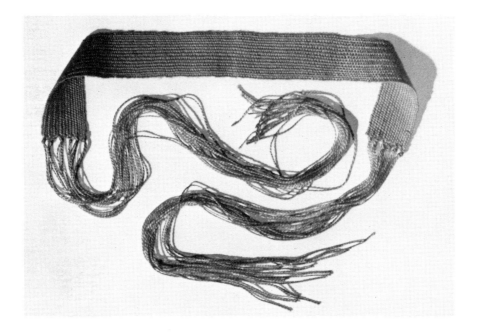

Warp the loom, following directions on p. 21, but measure off 21 inches of warp before putting in the warp sticks. Wind this extra warp around whatever your weaving is tied to. If you would like a wider belt, spread the warps a little farther apart.

Plain weave for 21 inches.

When removing the belt from the loom, do not cut the

51

warp. Just untie the knots at both ends and remove the harness.

Tie the fringe with overhand knots. It will measure about 24 inches long. Even if it is not the same length on both ends, you do not need to cut it. This way you can use all of the warp with no waste.

BELT WITH BUCKLE

When you make this belt, the buckle acts as part of the loom, holding the warp threads tight. You may use any buckle that has a crossbar about 1 inch wide to which the warp threads can be attached.

Warp: Wool yarn (red)
      6 threads, 90 inches long (these will be folded in half and used double)
Weft: Wool yarn (red)
Amount needed: 2 ounces
Finished size: 1 inch wide, waist measurement plus 5 inches long

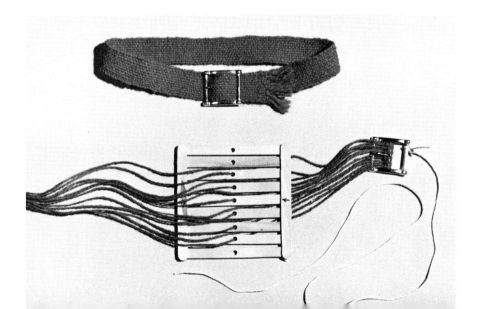

Put the warp on the crossbar of the buckle with snitch knots (p. 14). (You will have 12 warp threads, each 45 inches long.)

Put the warp threads through the harness. Attach the buckle to something firm either by placing it over something like a hook or by tying it to something with string. Comb through the warp threads. Tie the other end of the warp with an overhand knot and fasten it to a firm spot. The warp should be pulled tight. Do not use warp sticks.

Starting at the buckle, work plain weave. When the belt is as long as you want, cut the warp, leaving enough to tie for the fringe.

SHAG RUG

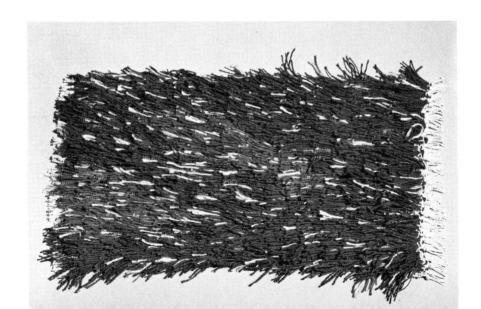

Warp: Cotton string
      17 threads, 1½ yards long, for each strip (total — 119 threads)

Weft: Cotton string and yarn (wool or synthetic). Any kind or color will do for this weft, as it will be hidden by the knots. This is a good chance to use up yarn you do not like.

Knots: Wool yarn and rayon yarn. Choose colors that you like. The knots in the picture were made with blue wool, red wool, red rayon, white rayon, and green rayon. Most of the knots were combinations of these colors. Thrums (leftover warps) or odds and ends may be used.

Amounts needed: Depends on size of rug. Start with a small ball of string.

Finished size: 14 inches wide, 25 inches long (including fringe)

This rug is made from seven 2-inch strips that are sewed together.

For the knots, cut pieces of yarn 4 to 5 inches long. Measure the yarn with a ruler, several threads at a time, or wind it around a piece of cardboard or your fingers to get the length that you want. Do not try to make them exactly the same length, because you want a shag effect.

For each strip, warp the loom (p. 21) with cotton string. Using string as weft, plain weave for ½ inch. Change to yarn weft and plain weave for 1 inch.

Following directions on p. 42, work one row of knots, using three threads in each knot.

Continue to work 1 inch of plain weave and one row of knots until the strip measures 22½ inches. Change to string weft and work ½ inch of plain weave.

Cut the strip from the loom and tie the warp ends to form fringe.

Work six more strips following the same directions. As you work, check the new weaving against the finished strips to make sure the colors will blend.

Sew the strips together, following directions below. If you do not want the fringe to show, just fold it to the wrong side and sew it down.

TO JOIN TWO PIECES OF FABRIC: Pin the two pieces together, right (or wrong) sides together, or place them side by side. Thread a tapestry needle with yarn or string to match the weaving. To thread the needle easily, fold back a piece of the thread and put the fold through the eye.

Tie an overhand knot at the end of the thread.

Sew the pieces together with an overhand stitch, as shown. Leave the stitches loose enough so that the pieces will lie flat.

The sewing may be done on the right or wrong side, whichever looks better.

PILLOWS

Warp: Cotton and rayon yarn (yellow)
      17 threads, 1 yard long, for each strip (total – 85 threads for each pillow)
Weft: Cotton and rayon yarn (yellow)
Amount needed: 4 ounces for each pillow
Finished size: 11 inches wide, 11 inches long

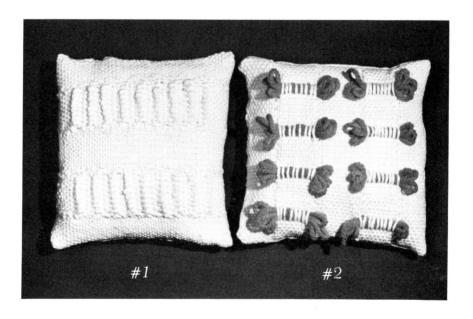

#1   #2

Each of these pillows is made from five separate strips. To make either pillow, you will also need a piece of material 12 inches square in a color that goes with your pillow front, and a pillow to go inside. If you use a separate pillow inside, instead of putting stuffing directly into the woven cover, you will be able to remove the cover easily for cleaning. You can buy a pillow the right size, or you can make one from two 12-inch squares of material. Sew around the edges of the squares, leaving an opening. Turn the case inside out; stuff with foam rubber, Dacron filling, or other soft material; and sew up the opening.

For pillow #2, you will also need eight 1-yard pieces of yarn in a contrasting color.

Pillow #1

Warp loom (p. 21). Work plain weave for 12 inches. Before removing the strip from the loom, put a thin line of white glue along each end of the strip. This will keep the ends from raveling, so you do not need to tie knots.

Make two more strips the same way.

Warp loom. Work 2 inches of plain weave, then one row of loops (see p. 38). Then work three rows of plain weave. Repeat one row of loops and three rows of plain weave until you have nine rows of loops. Then work 2 inches of plain weave. Your strip will be about 12 inches long and will look like the picture. (For a different effect, you might want to try leaving only one row of plain weave between the rows of loops; you will need seventeen rows of loops).

Make one more strip the same way.

Sew the five strips together to look like the picture, following the directions on p. 55.

Take the 12-inch square of matching material and put it on top of the woven square, right sides together. Pin the pieces together along three sides with straight pins. Baste along these sides and stitch with a sewing machine or by hand. Turn the pillow cover right side out, put the pillow inside, and close the open side by sewing it together by hand. If you prefer, you can sew on snaps, a zipper, or buttons instead.

Pillow #2

Make three 12-inch strips of plain weave, as for pillow #1.

For the decorated strips, warp the loom and work plain weave for 2 inches. Take a 1-yard piece of contrasting yarn. Spread the fingers of your left hand a little bit apart and wind the yarn loosely around your left hand. Slide the yarn off your hand, holding it in the middle, which should be where the ends are. You should have a little bundle of yarn about 4 inches long, with four loops at each end. Insert this into the next shed.

Change shed and work plain weave for 2 inches. Put in another bundle of contrasting yarn. Repeat this twice more, then finish the strip with 2 inches of plain weave. It should look like the picture.

Make another strip following these same directions.

Join the strips and finish the pillow following the directions for pillow #1.

The Backstrap Loom: Beams to Hold the Warp

Up to this point you have held your warp threads by tying them together. Another way to hold the warp threads is by tying them to sticks. Sticks used this way are called *beams*. If the warp is put on beams, it is easy to space the threads evenly and to adjust the tension. The beams also make it possible to space the warps farther apart. If you want to weave wider fabric, you will need a wider harness (p. 68), and you will have to put the warp on beams.

Any kind of firm sticks will do, but dowels work well. Dowels are round sticks. They come in different sizes, measured by diameter, which is the measurement across the center of the dowel. They are generally 36 inches long. A ¼-inch dowel will cost about twelve cents. If you use the large harness, you might want to buy the next size dowel, ⅜ inch, which will be stronger.

With a saw, cut the dowel into three pieces, each 12 inches long. If you do not have a saw, break the dowel by pressing it down across the edge of a table and smooth the ends with sandpaper.

You will need two 12-inch beams. Use a ruler to find the center of each beam and mark it with a pencil.

The beam to which the warp is tied first is called the *warp beam.* The warp threads are put on the warp beam with snitch knots.

Since the warp will be put on the beams double, each warp thread should be twice as long as the warp you will need. For the small harness (nine heddles) on

59

which you made the sample, you need seventeen warp threads. To put the warp on beams, you will need eight double warps (2 yards long) and one single warp, which should be a little more than a yard long, as it will be tied onto the warp beam. This will give you seventeen warp threads, each 1 yard long.

TO PUT THE WARP ON BEAMS

1. If you have an odd number of warp threads, you will have one single warp. Tie the single warp at the center mark of one beam with two half hitches. This will be the warp beam.

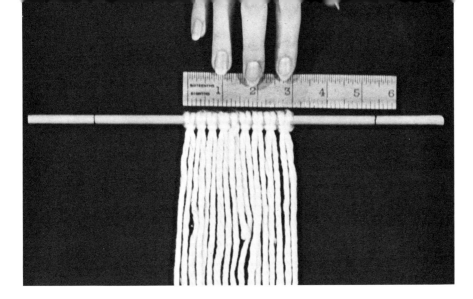

2. Put half of the double warps on each side of the center with snitch knots. If you want your warp to be 3 inches wide, measure to see that the outside warp on each side is 1¹/₂ inches away from the center mark. The threads should be spaced evenly.

3. Tape the warp firmly to the beam with masking tape. Tie a piece of heavy string to both ends of the beam, an equal distance from the center, with two half hitches. Tape the string into place.

Tie or tape the string to something sturdy, so you will be able to pull the warp firmly. Or tape the whole beam to something firm.

4. Put the warp through the harness. Start by putting the single middle warp thread through the middle heddle. Now work outward from the center, keeping the warp threads in the same order that they are on the warp beam.

5. The second beam, to which the front end of the warp is attached, is called the *front beam*. Tie a piece of heavy string about a yard long to one end of the front beam. Tape it into place.

6. Put the string around your waist and tie it to the other end of the beam. Do not tape this second end, as you will need to take it off when you stop working and put it on again later. This kind of loom, with a strap around the waist, is called a *backstrap loom*.

7. With the front beam fastened to your waist, you are ready to tie the warp to it. Take two warp threads in each hand. Make sure these threads are next to each other on the warp beam. Place them over the top of the front beam, then take them under the beam and bring them around and up as shown.

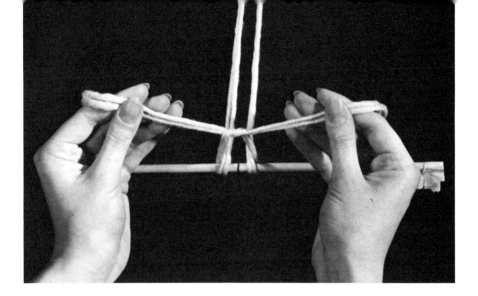

8. Tie them together with an overhand knot.

9. Then tie a half bowknot.

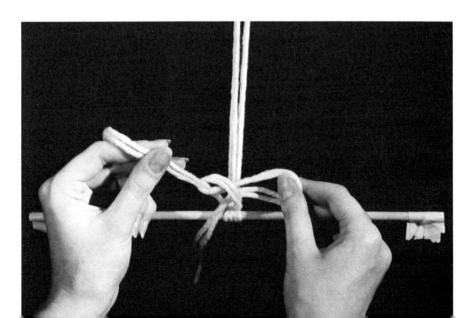

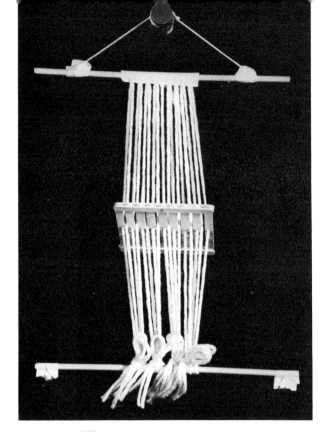

Repeat steps 7, 8, and 9 to attach the remaining warp ends. You will have four sets of knots, one of which will contain five threads. The warp should be the same width along the front beam as along the warp beam and spaced evenly from the center mark.

10. Put in four warp sticks (as in the practice piece) and you are ready to begin weaving.

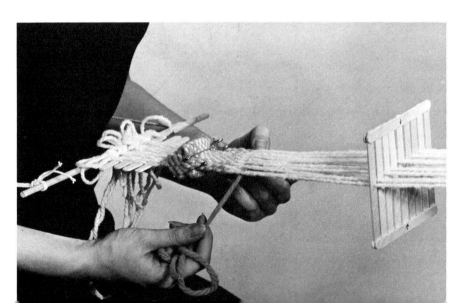

When you use the backstrap, you are part of the loom. You control the tension of the warp by leaning back to keep it tight.

When the fabric gets too long to weave comfortably, fold it and pin it securely with safety pins.

Collect all the things you will need before you start to weave. The butterfly (or butterflies), comb (beater), ruler, scissors, and safety pins should be within easy reach.

WALL HANGING

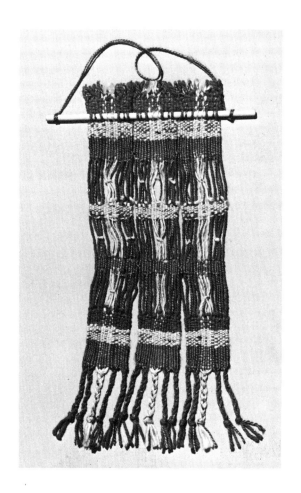

Warp: Wool yarn (red), rayon yarn (red and white)
      17 threads for each strip (total—51):
          12 double warps, 2 yards long (red wool)
          6 double warps, 2 yards long (red rayon)
          3 single warps, 40 inches long (red rayon)
Weft: Wool yarn (red), rayon yarn (red and white)
Amounts needed: 1 ounce red wool, 1 ounce red rayon, 1 ounce
      white rayon
Finished size: 15 inches long, 6 inches wide

Wool and rayon yarn are used together in this wall hanging for an interesting texture. They should be about the same weight. To hang it up, you will also need a dowel 9 inches long.

The wall hanging is made in three strips, which are then joined.

For each strip, put warp threads on a warp beam in this order, following directions on p. 60. Attach the single red rayon warp in the center. On either side attach a white rayon double warp. Next to these attach a red wool double warp on each side. Next, attach a red rayon double warp on each side. Attach a red wool double warp at each end. The end threads should each be 1 inch from the center mark; the whole warp should be 2 inches wide.

Tape warp into place. Thread warp through harness, with the single warp through the middle heddle. Keep the double threads in the same order. Attach warp to front beam, keeping warp 2 inches wide.

For weft, make a butterfly of each kind of yarn.

Plain weave with red rayon weft for 1 inch, white rayon weft for 1/2 inch, red wool weft for 1/2 inch.

Finish the last row as if you were ending the weaving, turning in the end of the weft. Then measure off 2 inches of warp which will be empty space with no weaving.

Starting after those 2 inches, work plain weave with red rayon weft for ½ inch; end off and leave another 2-inch space.

Work plain weave with white rayon weft for ½ inch; end off and leave another 2-inch space.

Work plain weave with red rayon weft for ¾ inch, then with white rayon weft for ½ inch, and end off.

Change shed and insert a stick. Leave the stick in place as you continue to weave.

Change shed. Work plain weave with red wool weft for ½ inch. End off.

Take short pieces of white rayon yarn and tie them around groups of threads in the middle of the 2-inch spaces. Tie with square knots and trim ends close to knots. You can tie them in any arrangement you like. In the picture the two side strips are tied differently from the middle one.

Remove the strip from the loom. Tie square knots in the warp threads at the top. Finish the bottom with 3-inch braids ending in overhand knots. The middle braid will have five threads.

Work two more strips, following these same directions.

Cut a dowel 9 inches long and smooth the ends with sandpaper. Remove the sticks and put the dowel through the three strips where the sticks were. Thread a tapestry needle with red rayon yarn. Join the strips together at two places, right above the first 2-inch space and the last 2-inch space, by taking one stitch into two strips from the wrong side and tying off the ends with a square knot. Trim ends closely.

Making a Larger Harness

To make wider fabric, you will need a larger harness. The two harnesses in the picture are made the same way as the small harness.

The smaller one (*a*) is made by joining two small harnesses with extra sticks, front and back.

The larger harness (*b*) is used for the projects that follow. The long sticks for the top and bottom are balsa wood, which can be bought in a hobby shop. It is a very lightweight thin wood that is easy to cut with scissors. It comes in pieces 36 inches long that cost about twenty cents. Buy two pieces ½ inch wide.

Cut both pieces of balsa wood in half. You will have four strips, each 18 inches long.

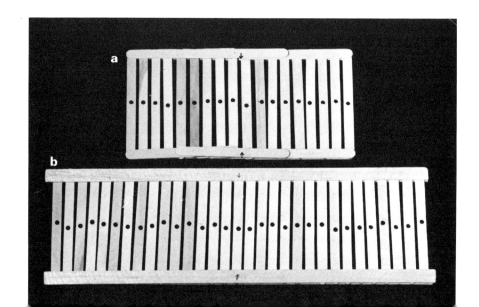

Make holes in 31 sticks and smooth the sticks with sandpaper. Glue them to the balsa wood strips, spacing them the same distance apart, as you did for the small harness. The 31 sticks in the picture covered 15 inches of the balsa wood. Your harness may be a little shorter or longer. After the sticks are glued into place, just cut off the extra balsa and smooth the ends with sandpaper.

Mark the center of the harness with arrows.

SCARF

Warp: Knitting worsted (white)
      61 threads (use large harness):
         30 double warps, 4 yards long
           1 single warp, 76 inches long
Weft : Bulky yarn (red)
Amounts needed: 2 ounces red, 2 ounces white
Finished size: 8 inches wide, 58 inches long (including fringe)

Put warp threads on warp beam, following directions on p. 60. Tie the single warp at the center mark. Space the double warps evenly. The width of the warp should be 8 inches; check to see that the outside warp on each side is 4 inches from the center. Tape warp into place. Thread it through the large harness and tie to front beam. The warp must also be 8 inches wide on the front beam (4 inches from center mark on each side).

You will need warp sticks to spread the warp evenly, but the small sticks will be too short. Instead, you may use two ¼-inch dowels, each 12 inches long.

Work plain weave for 42 inches.

Remove weaving from loom. Knot the fringe with overhand knots and trim it evenly. The fringe on the scarf in the picture is 8 inches long.

SHOULDER BAG

Warp: Wool weaving yarn (blue, gray, and red)
      61 threads (use large harness):
         30 double warps, 3 yards long
          1 single warp, 58 inches long
Weft: Wool weaving yarn (blue)
Amount needed: 4 ounces (total)
Finished size: 8 inches wide, 10 inches long

Prepare the warp the same as for the scarf (p. 70), using 12-inch dowels as warp sticks. The warp should be 8 inches wide.

Work plain weave for 1 inch. Change shed. Put in a dowel and change shed again. Leave this dowel in the fabric. It will be removed at the end of the weaving to leave a space for the drawstring to go through.

Work plain weave for 18 inches. Change shed. Put in a second dowel. Change shed.

Work plain weave for 1 inch.

Remove weaving from loom. Leave the sticks in place. Tie overhand knots in the fringe, five threads at a time. Trim fringe to 3 inches long.

Fold the weaving in half, with fringed ends together. Pin sides together evenly. Thread a tapestry needle with yarn and sew up both sides, following directions on p. 55.

Using 3 threads of each color, make a braid 54 inches long to use as a drawstring, and two braids each 14 inches long to trim the sides. End off the braids with overhand knots.

Pin a 14-inch braid along each side, leaving the extra length at the bottom. Sew into place, using a tapestry needle. Retie bottom overhand knots even with bottom of bag, as shown.

Remove sticks and pull drawstring braid through spaces left by the sticks. Untie the knots at the ends of the drawstring and tie them together with one overhand knot.

PLASTIC PLACE MAT

Warp: Cotton string (blue); plain white string may be used instead
      61 threads (use large harness):
         30 double warps, 45 inches long
          1 single warp, 25 inches long
Weft: Cotton string (blue) and plastic strips (see directions below)
Amounts needed: 60 yards cotton string, 3 plastic bread bags
Finished size: 11 inches wide, 18 inches long (including fringe)

Warp the loom the same way as for the scarf (p. 70). The warp should be 12 inches wide. (It will pull in a little as you weave.)

Prepare two butterflies, one string and one plastic.

With string weft, plain weave for ½ inch, ending with butterfly at right. Change shed. Beat.

Weave one row of plastic weft, ending with weft at right. Change shed. Beat.

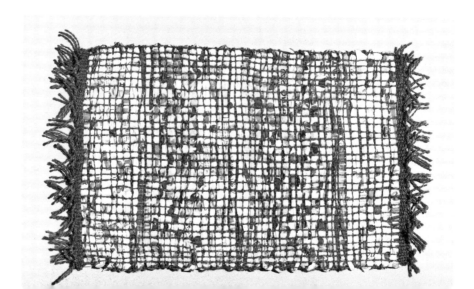

Cross the string weft over the plastic weft and pass the string weft from right to left. Change shed. Beat.

Pass plastic weft from right to left. Change shed. Beat.

Continue to weave, crossing wefts at both selvages. Work until piece measures 15½ inches.

With string weft alone, plain weave for ½ inch.

Remove weaving from loom. Tie warp ends, four at a time, with square knots. Trim fringe to 1 inch.

TO CUT PLASTIC STRIPS: Cut into a plastic bag at an angle until strip is 2 inches wide. With one hand inside the bag, cut around and around, keeping the strip 2 inches wide. Use a ruler to measure as you go along. A rubber band around the 2-inch mark will be a helpful guide. One bread bag will make a strip of plastic about 4 or 5 yards long.

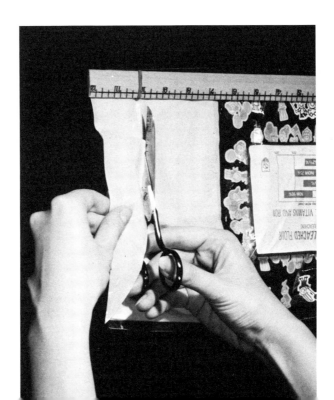

BLUE JEAN RUG

Warp: Cotton string
   61 threads for each section (use large harness):
    60 double warps, 3½ yards long
     2 single warps, 67 inches long
Weft: Cotton string and strips of fabric (see directions below)
Amounts needed: Start with 1 ball of string, one pair discarded
   blue jeans (or scraps)
Finished size: 30 inches long, 20 inches wide (including fringe)

 This rug is made in two sections joined together.
 Put warp on warp beam, following directions on p. 60.
Warp should be 10 inches wide.
 Prepare two butterflies, one string and one fabric.
 With string weft, plain weave for 1 inch.
 Change to fabric weft and plain weave until piece is
25 inches long.
 Change to string weft and plain weave for 1 inch.
 Cut weaving from loom. Tie warp threads with over-
hand knots, four at a time. Trim fringe to 2 inches.
 Make another section following these same direc-
tions.

Sew the sections together by hand, following directions on p. 55, or by machine.

TO CUT STRIPS OF FABRIC: It is best to cut the fabric along the warp (length of jeans). Cut along a straight thread and make the strips 3 inches wide. Do not use worn spots or heavy seams. Fold each strip into thirds, so it is 1 inch wide, and press with an iron. Each half of this rug used about thirteen of these strips. Each strip wove about three rows.

To add a new strip, overlap it with the end of the strip before, following the same directions as for yarn.

An old pair of blue jeans was used for the rug in the picture, but scraps of any material, old or new, may be used.

The Beginner Loom

To make this loom, buy a piece of 2 × 8 lumber 30 inches long and a 1-inch dowel 36 inches long. The wood will probably cost under $2.00.

Measure 3 inches from each end of the base. Measure to find the center points of these lines. Use a drill with a 1-inch bit to drill a hole through the board at these spots.

Cut the dowel in half. Each piece will be 18 inches long. Fit the two dowels into the holes in the base.

Use sandpaper to get all the parts smooth. The loom may be painted if you like.

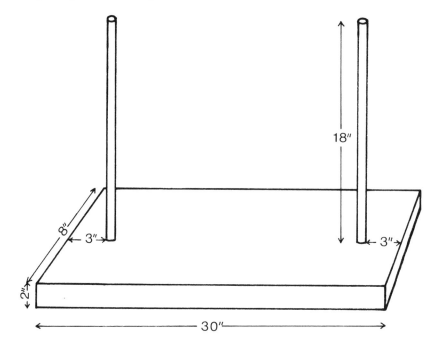

Helpful Hints

Rough sticks can catch the threads, so use sandpaper to sand all the sticks smooth, including the dowels. If a dowel is used for a hanging, sand the two ends also. Tape a piece of sandpaper to a flat stick for easier handling. An emery board may be used instead.

To measure warp, put the ball of yarn or string into a large paper bag. This will keep it from rolling on the floor while you are measuring it. If you are using more than one color of warp, put all the balls into the bag and measure them at the same time.

You may have an even or an odd number of warp threads.

When you thread the heddles (put the warp threads through), fold the end of the warp and put the fold through the eye.

A crochet hook is helpful in tying knots and in threading string heddles.

When the warp has been prepared, plan to do the whole piece of weaving at one time, if possible. Your fabric will be more even. If you do not finish the weaving, loosen the warp until you are ready to go on. It is not good to keep the warp stretched.

Don't make a butterfly too big to pass easily through the shed. Four or five yards will make a good size.

You may weave either standing or sitting, whichever you find more comfortable.

Never leave an end of weft at the selvage. Always turn it back into the weaving for at least three warps.

To keep the fabric even, measure it as you weave. Push the harness away from the weaving to get an accurate measurement.

When tying knots in the warp threads to form the fringe, try to get the knots as close to the fabric as possible. Start with the knot loose and tighten it as you push it close to the fabric.

If you do not want fringe on your fabric, tie the knots just the same. Cut the fringe short, turn it to the wrong side of the fabric, and sew it in place by hand.

Woven fabrics generally come off the loom flat and straight. However, if you want to press a woven article, or if the fringe needs pressing, follow these directions. Press lightly on the wrong side, using a steam iron over a dry cloth. With a plain iron, use a damp cloth.

Glossary

backstrap loom	a loom that is attached to the weaver by means of a string, a piece of fabric, or a strap
beam	the part of the loom to which the warp threads are attached. A loom has two beams, a warp beam and a front beam
beat	to push the weft into place
beater	anything used to beat the weft, such as a comb
butterfly	weft yarn made into a form that can be passed easily through the shed
change shed	raise or lower the harness
dowel	a round stick
eye	hole or opening, as in a heddle or a needle
fabric	woven material
fibers	tiny fine threads that are twisted together to form thread or yarn
front beam	the beam close to the weaver, to which the warp threads are tied
hank	a coil or skein of yarn
harness	a frame that raises and lowers sets of warp threads
heddle	one of a set of vertical sticks or strings with an eye in the middle; part of the harness
loom	a device for weaving yarn or thread into fabric
ply	to twist or spin two or more threads together; also, the small threads that are twisted together

selvage	the "self edge" along the side of a woven fabric
shed	the space formed when a set of warp threads is raised or lowered; the weft passes through the shed
skein	a coil of yarn
slit	the space between two heddles
spin	to twist fibers together to form string, thread, or yarn
synthetic	man-made
tabby	plain weave
tension	tightness
thread	twisted fibers of any kind
thrums	warp threads left on the loom after the weaving is cut off
warp	the lengthwise threads of a fabric
warp beam	the beam at the back of a loom to which the warp threads are tied
warp stick	a stick put into the shed to keep the warp threads straight
weft	the crosswise threads of a fabric